Love
and
blessings
to whomever
finds this
book!

Love,
JOJO
♡ ☺

Buddy the Bunny's Perfect Day

 An original publication of DreamsGiveHope

Created, written, and edited by JoAnnA Perkin
Character development by JoAnnA Perkin
Artistic portion of character development by Marius Holmes
Illustrated by Catherine Buckels (with facilitations by Singularity House)
Modifications made by Brooklyn Printing Company

ISBN-13: 978-0615967554
ISBN-10: 0615967558
LCCN: 2014903015

Discover more at:
Buddythebunnybooks.com
info@buddythebunnybooks.com

Families flourish with books from DreamsGiveHope

Dear Parent/Teacher:

As an educator and passionate child advocate for the last seventeen years with a Master's in Education, I am elated to introduce Buddy the Bunny's Perfect Day—the first book in my classic children's series. Each of my eight characters symbolizes one of Gardner's multiple intelligences, where the focus is not on how intelligent an individual is, but rather, "how many ways one is intelligent." The multiple intelligence theory abandons the old premise that limits intelligence to only two intelligences (linguistic and mathematical) that have been traditionally valued in modern secular schools, and conceives intelligence as multiple rather than unitary in nature. In other words, there are a myriad of ways one may be intelligent outside of what we have been conditioned. Einstein had it right in the fifties when he said, "Everyone is a genius. But if you judge a fish on its ability to climb a tree, it will live its whole life believing it is stupid."

Buddy the Bunny Series targets ages 3 and up (pre-school and beyond). It is timeless as opposed to trendy—going back to the basics and good ole-fashioned values, while maintaining edgy aesthetics and a storyline that still appeals to the modern child. In addition to incorporating the multiple intelligences through each of the eight characters, my series is replete with life lessons such as the importance of friendship, learning from mistakes, cooperation, serving others, gratitude, perseverance, courage, and reciprocity. Unlike the average children's book, the elements of plot are evident in each piece within my series. Buddy the Bunny also introduces young readers to descriptive vocabulary, internal rhyme/assonance, alliteration, onomatopoeia, etc., making it applicable in the educational arena as well as with parents.

Here's to your child flourishing in a friendship with Buddy the Bunny!

Sincerely,

JoAnnA Perkin
Creator/Editor in Chief

A very special

thank you

to Marius Holmes

for his artistic ability

to originally capture

the vibrant images of

Buddy and friends that

I've held in my heart for the last ten years!

This
DreamsGiveHope book
belongs to

The sun shone in and Buddy awoke.
He had been dreaming of pouncing on
the court playing tennis. It was the
serve to determine the winning point.
It had been a very challenging game
and now . . .

Beaver returned the ball–back and
forth, back and forth–POW!!! The
winning point! Buddy the Bunny is the Cham–pi–on!

This was the day Buddy was waiting
for—a tennis match with Beaver!

On the court, Buddy stretched in bliss,
while he awaited Beaver's arrival.

Crash-boom-bang!!!! Buddy heard the commotion, and looked to see Beaver with his racket and tennis balls all in a tussle,

and him hanging hammock-style out of the tennis net!

"Now then, allow me to compose
myself," Beaver took a deep breath.
"Yes, yes, I feel adequately prepared.
Shall we begin?"

Soon enough they were playing tennis,
but Beaver spent more time tripping over
his tail than actually hitting the ball.

The score: 40/love, Buddy's lead.

Still, Buddy was not happy.

This game was far too easy.

Buddy didn't understand. Beaver *talked* such a good game.
He had such a vast knowledge of tennis.

Buddy couldn't help wishing he were skating with Roller Rooster.

"Beaver," Buddy exclaimed impatiently. "You have to follow through to get the ball to cross where you want it to cross!"

"Whatever do you mean?" Beaver questioned quite offended. "I happen to be very well-versed in the genre of tennis and in a plethora of other sports as well."

9

"Would you speak English," Buddy
requested extremely perturbed
and shaking his head.

"Is my language too copious for your
diminutive comprehension?"
Beaver asked with a superior smirk.

"I'm not sure what you just said, Beaver,
but I am sure of one thing--your tennis game
needs a lot of work," Buddy responded.

"Well," Beaver replied insulted, his head
held haughty and dignified while he
began to gather his things, and once again
tripping over his tail, "Perhaps you should
seek an individual with superior
physical coordination such as yourself. I didn't
ask to be born with such a disproportionately
large tail not suited in a fashion necessary for
many sophisticated, sporty endeavors."

Beaver, in an attempt to exit gracefully,
tripped on his tail once again.

Buddy began to feel bad, so he decided
to make things right.

"Beaver, just because we don't play
tennis together well, doesn't mean we
can't hang out and do other things.
Why don't we go visit Wolfus?!
He has a new pool!"

"I suppose if he has a raft, I could relax
and do a crossword puzzle,"
Beaver replied, his anger fading quickly.

"That's the spirit,"
Buddy smiled and bounced.

And . . .

They were off on the trail to Wolfus'
house singing along the way.

"Fee-fi-fum-fo . . . we're off to the pool, oh."

"Gonna do laps and play water polo!"

"We're off to the pool, oh."

"Gonna beat your tail in splashy tag."

"I'm gonna be reading my poetry mag!"

"Fee-fi-fum-fo . . . we're off to the pool, oh."

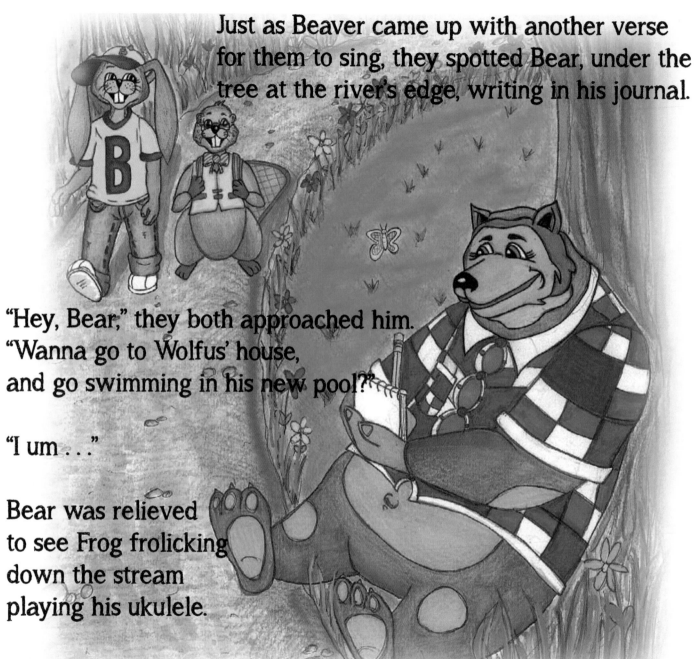

Just as Beaver came up with another verse for them to sing, they spotted Bear, under the tree at the river's edge, writing in his journal.

"Hey, Bear," they both approached him. "Wanna go to Wolfus' house, and go swimming in his new pool?"

"I um . . ."

Bear was relieved to see Frog frolicking down the stream playing his ukulele.

"I bet Frog would love to go," Bear said elated to get back to his journal writing.

16

"Yes!" Frog exclaimed.
"I would love to go!"

And . . .

Beaver, Frog, and Buddy continued on the path to Wolfus' house.

Now, with Frog on the scene, they had a melody to complement their song.

"Fee-fi-fum . . ."

"Isn't that Owler?"
Beaver questioned Buddy.

"It looks like it!" Buddy exclaimed
on his return swing from Mr. Willow.

"What exactly is he doing?" Frog questioned.

19

The three of them walked over to Owler and found him, with measuring tape, winging back and forth between tree branches.

"I'm interested to know, Owler, whatever is it that is engaging you so?" Beaver inquired.

Owler, suddenly thrown from his deep concentration, was so startled his glasses went flying!

"He's getting there! He's almost there! He's ready to get it! Annnnd . . . he catches it! You're out of there!!!"

Buddy is on his back, dust flying, like he had just made the winning catch in a very important baseball game.

21

"May I have my glasses back?
I was just in the middle of measuring
the distance between six
tree branches," Owler squinted.

Buddy tossed him his glasses.

"We were wondering,"
Frog continued strumming his ukulele.

"We would have the merriest time . . .
if you accompanied us to Wolfus'
house to go swimming in his new
pool," Beaver finished.

"What is the length of the pool?" Owler questioned with interest and enthusiasm.

"Who cares! It's a pool and pools are made for swimming, games, and just plain fun!" Buddy bounced exuberantly.

And . . .

Beaver, Frog, Owler, and Buddy were
back on the trail to Wolfus' house.

Buddy began kicking rocks between two trees.
For now, he was a soccer star!!!

Just as he thought he found the perfect rock . . .

"Oh nooo, HEEEEEEEEEELP!"

It was turtle—his binoculars, sunglasses, and butterfly net flying in the air!

Buddy, with his quick reflexes,
jumped in the air and caught Turtle.

Turtle was quite relieved, and
Beaver, Frog, and Owler were
entertained, laughing until
their bellies hurt.

"I almost caught the most beautiful
Monarch butterfly. Orange and black markings
are my favorite," Turtle said
putting on his sunglasses.

"We're going to Wolfus' to swim in his new pool.
Wanna come with us?"
Owler flapped his wings in excitement.

Turtle with a squint of skepticism, "I don't know . . .
Does he put chemicals in his pool?"

"He has a natural filtration system,
of course," Beaver replied confidently.

And . . .

Beaver, Frog, Owler, Turtle, and Buddy
were back on the trail to Wolfus' house.

Soon it was dusk, and the group had not yet arrived.

"It seems as if we have had adequate time to have already arrived at Wolfus' house," Beaver said with concern.

"Yes, according to my estimate, we have been traveling for two hours, twenty-six minutes, and fifty-seven seconds just since I joined the group," Owler added looking at his watch.

29

"Beaver, Owler didn't join us until after Frog," Buddy said a little worried.

"We just need to find the wishing well. It's right around the corner. I found some great tadpoles there last month," Turtle said.

"We really should pick up the pace. I would like to be able to see the piano keys and develop this new melody that I want to finish," urged Frog.

"Did I hear the five of you are lost?" Buckly the Buck suddenly appeared.

He had been painting what he believed to be one of his most brilliant pieces.

"Buckly!" they exclaimed in unison.

"We're saved," Buddy bounced, relieved and with renewed hope.

31

"Follow me," Buckly directed. "The sun's location reveals that we should be moving southwest. If we're swift, we can make it before dark."

Sure enough, Buckly got them there quickly.

"You guys must have read my mind," Wolfus glowed. "Come around to the back. Let's have a party, and I'll bring out the beach balls and snacks."

They all went back to the pool.

And . . .

Turtle chased fireflies,
letting them go,
of course, and
delighting in their magic.

Beaver told
all sorts of
interesting
stories and
hilarious jokes.

Frog hammed it up
on the piano, clinging
and clanging
in musical delight.

Buckly worked comfortably on a jig-saw puzzle.

Buddy played between splashing around in the pool, and dancing the night away.

He was in heaven!

Owler happily tested the PH level in the pool— between Buddy's splishin and splashin, that is.

And Wolfus played the perfect host,
catching up on old times, while he passed out
homemade cookies and fresh-squeezed lemonade.

Beaver was in the middle of one of his
wild and crazy stories when . . .

Bear strolled in, journal in hand and deep in thought.

"Just when I thought things couldn't get any better, you go and make the night complete," Wolfus warmed.

"I have an idea," Buckly said abandoning his jig-saw puzzle. "Everyone get together for a picture!"

And . . .

They all gathered around, happy to be together.

"Say Cheese . . ."

Beaver, Bear, Frog, Owler, Turtle, Wolfus, and Buddy all smiled for
the camera under the magic of the stars.

The End

Made in the USA
Charleston, SC
27 April 2014